THE DNA OF JOY

FINDING JOY IN EVERYDAY LIFE

GREG SURRATT
seacoast church

TABLE OF CONTENTS

CONTENTS

Foreword by Shawn Wood   5
Introduction to The DNA of Joy   6
Using this Workbook   8
Session 1: The DNA of Joy   12
Session 2: The DNA of Relationships   22
Session 3: The DNA of a Great Bad Day   32
Session 4: The DNA of Perseverance   42
Session 5: The DNA of Contentment   52
Session 6: The DNA of Giving   62

APPENDIX

Frequently Asked Questions   74
Small Group Agreement   77
Small Group Calendar   79
Team Roles   80
Spiritual Partners' Check-In Page   82
Small Group Roster   83
Memory Verses   84
Prayer and Praise Report   85

SMALL GROUP LEADERS

Hosting an Open House   86
Leading for the First Time   87
Small Group Leadership 101 (Top Ten Ideas for New Hosts) 89

ABOUT THE AUTHOR

Pastor Greg Surratt   92

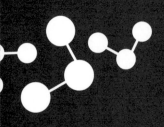

FOREWARD

"Joy" is a pretty common word. We sing "Joy to the World" at Christmastime. We have things in our lives that bring us joy and some that have stolen our joy. Maybe for some of us we even know someone named Joy.

As common a word as it is, I am not sure that I have always understood the real meaning of joy. I guess you could say that I've struggled to understand the DNA of joy.

Having the opportunity to rub shoulders with Greg Surratt for the past 12 years (10 years as a Pastor on staff at Seacoast Church), I got to see the DNA of joy lived out before my eyes.

I heard that DNA in the story of Greg as a young pastor planting a new church while at the same time facing a tragedy and nursing his daughter back from the brink of death. And yet, he found joy through it all. I saw this firsthand in the pastor who sat in his office after hearing a "no" from a local town council about building a new and bigger building. There was no happiness, but there was joy and it was joy that shot through the fog like a headlight to find the multi-site concept of church. I even sat on the phone with Greg as he walked me through the personal pain of losing a child to miscarriage and helped me through tears to count it all joy.

So with that experience as a backdrop, I cannot tell you how excited I am to have this resource to put into the hands of my church and to spread the word to as many churches as I can.

I am not sure where you are as you start this journey with your small group, but I do know this: after this study is complete you will have a better understanding of what makes up the DNA of Joy and what Jesus says about finding it. No matter where you are at this moment, you will be further along the journey to healing tomorrow than you are today. Your growth may seem slow at times, but it is the superhighway that leads to a joy that does not fade.

SHAWN WOOD
Founding Pastor, Freedom Church
Moncks Corner, SC

INTRODUCTION

TO THE DNA OF JOY

Hey Gang,

Welcome to The DNA of Joy! If this is your first small group experience, I want to welcome you in particular. Joining a small group is a big step, but I believe that it is one of the best decisions you can make. Everyone is different but one similarity we all share is the need for community. I think that you will discover (if you haven't already) the incredible value of learning to follow God with others.

I can remember how much fun it was to teach this series. When it was originally planned, The DNA of Joy was only supposed to last four weeks. After week one, I sat our team down and said, "This is a lot of fun! What if we made it a ten-week series?" That is exactly what we did and it ended up being one of the defining series of that year. We knew that we wanted to do more with The DNA of Joy and you are holding the result in your hands.

You and your group are going to spend the next six weeks learning about joy. I believe that we can learn a lot about joy from others. That is one of the reasons we knew The DNA of Joy would translate so well to a small group study. I can hear some of you now, "Do we really need six sessions to talk about joy?" Joy seems simple. The only thing is, if being joyful were easy, we would be that way all the time! I don't know about you, but my life could use a little more joy!

This study is about finding joy in everyday life. We find that joy through relationships, through generosity, through contentment, and more. By exploring these and other topics, my hope is that you and your group will encourage and challenge one another to pursue God in a way that you never have before. The joy God has for us is real and it is available to each one of us.

One more thing. Before we get started, I want to say thank you. I believe that one of the best ways to experience God is in the context of community. By joining or leading a group, you are committing to doing just that. I hope that your time together will be as impactful as any words in this study and that it brings all of you joy!

GREG SURRATT

USING THIS WORKBOOK

STUFF TO HELP YOU HAVE A GREAT SMALL GROUP EXPERIENCE

1 Notice in the Table of Contents there are three sections: (1) Sessions; (2) Appendix; and (3) Small Group Leaders. It will be helpful for you to get to know the Appendix sections. Some of them will be used in the sessions themselves.

2 If you are leading or co-leading a small group, the section for Small Group Leaders will give you some hard-learned experiences of others that will encourage you and help you avoid many common obstacles to effective small group leadership.

3 Use this workbook as a guide, not a straightjacket. If the group responds to the lesson in an unexpected but honest way, go with that. If you think of a better question than the next one in the lesson, ask it. Take to heart the insights included in the Frequently Asked Questions pages and the Small Group Leaders section.

4 Enjoy your small group experience!

5 Now check out the Outline of Each Session on the next pages so that you understand how the sessions will flow.

OUTLINE OF EACH SESSION

It can be easy for small groups to struggle with a very basic question: "what do we do when we meet?" That is why one of the goals of this study guide is to provide plenty of content and questions in an easy-to-follow format. We have tried to provide a good balance of teaching, practical exercises, worship, and ministry. By following these elements in your group time, your group will achieve a balance that is so important to healthy spiritual growth.

A typical group session for The DNA of Joy will include the following:

small talk.

We believe that one of the best places to learn about God is in community with people you know and trust. That's why each session will begin with a chance for your group to chat, share, and get everyone on the same page. This section typically offers you two options. You can get to know your whole group by using the icebreaker question(s), or you can provide an opportunity for one or two group members to share some of their thoughts or experiences.

As your group begins, use the Small Group Agreement, Small Group Calendar, and Team Roles to help your group see how everyone has a part in making a small group come to life. As the group grows closer together, use the Spiritual Partner's Check-In Page and the Prayer and Praise Report to keep the group connected.

teaching.

Serving as a companion to **The DNA of Joy** small group discussion book is **The DNA of Joy** video teaching. This DVD is designed to combine teaching segments from your pastors along with leadership insights and personal stories of life change. Using the teaching video will add value to this 6-week commitment of learning together and discovering how walking with Christ changes everything.

reflect.

Here is where you will process as a group the teaching you watched. We want your group to go beyond simply storing the information presented and instead consider: How should we live in light of the Word of God? We want to help you apply the insights from Scripture practically and creatively; to your heart as well as your head. At the end of the day, allowing the timeless truths from God's Word to transform our lives in Christ is our greatest aim.

respond.

This section is about your group learning how to practically apply the lessons you are learning together. We know that it is not simply enough to hear – we must take what we hear and make it a part of our everyday lives. But what does that look like? How can we do it? In this section, you'll have an opportunity to go beyond Bible study to biblical living. Your group will consider questions that are designed to help you think through the implications of what you are learning. The group session will close with time for personal response to God and group prayer, seeking to keep this crucial commandment before us at all times.

This is a good place to have different group members close in prayer, even when the instructions don't specify. You can also provide some time if the schedule allows for people to reflect on their Prayer and Praise Report or take a little time to meet with a Spiritual Partner.

going deeper.

If you have time and want to dig deeper into more Bible passages about the topic at hand, we've provided additional passages and questions. Your group may choose to do study homework ahead of each meeting in order to cover more biblical material. If you prefer not to do study homework, the Deeper Bible Study section will provide you with plenty to discuss within the group. These options allow individuals or the whole group to expand their study, while still accommodating those who can't do homework or are new to your group.

daily reflections.

Each week on the Daily Reflections pages we provide scriptures to read and reflect on between group meetings. We suggest you use this section to seek God on your own throughout the week. This time at home should begin and end with prayer. Don't get in a hurry; take enough time to hear God's direction.

memory verses.

For each session we have provided a memory verse that emphasizes an important truth from the session. This is an optional exercise, but we believe that memorizing Scripture can be a vital part of filling our minds with God's will for our lives. We encourage you to give this important habit a try.

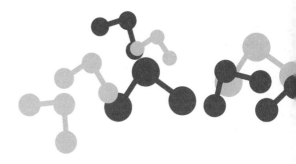

SESSION 1:
THE DNA OF JOY

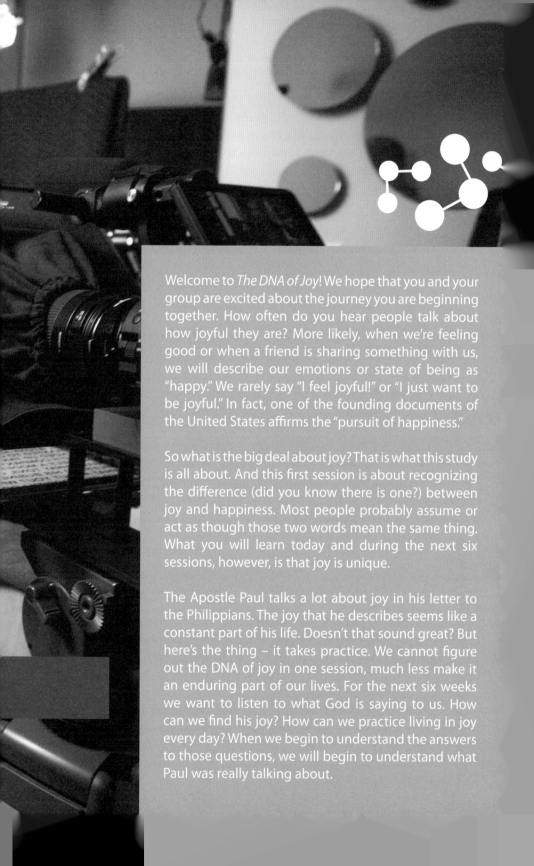

Welcome to *The DNA of Joy*! We hope that you and your group are excited about the journey you are beginning together. How often do you hear people talk about how joyful they are? More likely, when we're feeling good or when a friend is sharing something with us, we will describe our emotions or state of being as "happy." We rarely say "I feel joyful!" or "I just want to be joyful." In fact, one of the founding documents of the United States affirms the "pursuit of happiness."

So what is the big deal about joy? That is what this study is all about. And this first session is about recognizing the difference (did you know there is one?) between joy and happiness. Most people probably assume or act as though those two words mean the same thing. What you will learn today and during the next six sessions, however, is that joy is unique.

The Apostle Paul talks a lot about joy in his letter to the Philippians. The joy that he describes seems like a constant part of his life. Doesn't that sound great? But here's the thing – it takes practice. We cannot figure out the DNA of joy in one session, much less make it an enduring part of our lives. For the next six weeks we want to listen to what God is saying to us. How can we find his joy? How can we practice living in joy every day? When we begin to understand the answers to those questions, we will begin to understand what Paul was really talking about.

small TALK

During each session, we will begin with a question or brief activity designed to "put us on the same page" for the session. If this is your first time together, take a few minutes to make sure everyone knows each other's names. You may want to review briefly the Small Group Agreement and Calendar from the Appendix.

1 As you begin, take time to pass around a copy of the Small Group Roster on page 83, a sheet of paper, or one of your study guides opened to the Small Group Roster. Have everyone write down their contact information. Ask someone to make copies or type up a list with everyone's information and email it to the group this week.

2 Today we are going to examine the difference between joy and happiness. Do you think that there is a real difference? Take some time and discuss what those differences (if any) might be.

3 Whether your group is new or ongoing, it's always important to reflect on and review your values together. On pages 77 is a Small Group Agreement with the values we've found most useful in sustaining healthy, balanced groups. We recommend that you choose one or two values—ones you haven't previously focused on or ones that you have room to grow in—to emphasize during this study. Choose ones that will take your group to the next stage of intimacy and spiritual health.

If your group is new, you may want to focus on welcoming newcomers or on sharing group ownership. Any group will quickly move from being the leader's group to our group if everyone understands the goals of the group and shares a small role. See the Team Roles on page 80 for help on how to do this well.

We recommend that you rotate host homes on a regular basis and let the hosts lead the meeting. We have found that healthy groups rotate leadership. This helps to develop every member's ability to shepherd a few people in a safe environment. Even Jesus gave others the opportunity to serve alongside him (Mark 6:30–44). Look at the FAQs on page 74 for additional information about hosting or leading the group.

TEACHING

During each session in *The DNA of Joy* we're going to be hearing some teaching from Pastor Greg Surratt and learning what it means to find joy in everyday life. In his letter to the Philippians, Paul encourages his readers to be joyful at all times. In our culture, we tend to think in terms of "happiness" rather than "joy." But there is a difference between the two and we will explore that now:

PLAY DVD SESSION 1

Use the space below for notes, questions, or comments you want to bring up in the discussion later.

_____

_____

_____

_____

_____

_____

_____

_____

_____

_____

_____

_____

_____

_____

_____

_____

_____

_____

_____

REFLECT

1 At the beginning of the session, Greg asked if you had ever experienced buyer's remorse. As you think about your own life does anything stand out to you as a moment or experience where you thought you would be happy, but you ended up with buyer's remorse instead?

2 Greg's first point was that "happiness is what happens to you; joy is what is produced in you." Can you think of examples that illustrate each of those truths?

3 Paul says in Philippians 1:11 that we should try to "always be filled with the fruit of your salvation." Greg pointed out that in Galatians, Paul lists joy as one of the spiritual gifts we receive as believers. Then, in Philippians 4:4, Paul tells us to "Always be full of joy in the Lord." Does being full of joy all the time seem impossible to you? Why?

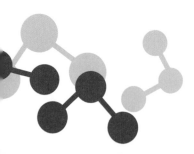

4 Think about your life – what made you happy when you were a child? How about as a teenager? A young adult? What about right now? Has the definition of what it takes to make you happy changed? Greg cited a verse from Proverbs that said "Human desire is never satisfied." Why do you think that is the case? What would it take to satisfy our desires?

RESPOND

Now it's time to make some personal applications to all we've been thinking about in the last few minutes.

1 In general, is your life characterized by the pursuit of joy, or happiness?

2 Is there an area in your life where insecurity drives a pursuit of happiness? What would it take to make you feel secure in God in that area?

3 What stood out to you most in this session? Where did God draw your attention? What changes might He be challenging you to make in your own life when it comes to recognizing the difference between joy and happiness.

4 Allow everyone to answer this question: "How can we pray for you this week?" Be sure to write prayer requests on your Prayer and Praise Report on page 85.

Close the session in prayer. Encourage each other to pray audibly for others in the group.

going DEEPER

Read Philippians 2:1-11 and John 15:10-11. In the Philippians passage, Paul gives us a beautiful picture of what Jesus did for us by coming to earth as a man. He humbled himself and endured the cross. Yet in John 15:10-11, we see that Jesus wanted his followers to have the same sort of joy that he did:

1 The passages say that Jesus was full of joy, even though he had given up all of his rights and privileges to come and be one of us. Could you be joyful in the midst of such sacrifice?

2 Philippians 2:1-11 talks about being humble, considering others as better than ourselves, and looking out for the interests of others. Our culture tends to reject these things as paths to happiness. Why?

3 Having read and reflected on these passages, how would you describe the joy that Jesus had? What made it distinct from happiness as we tend to understand it?

daily REFLECTIONS

These are daily reviews of the key Bible verses and related others that will help you think about and apply the insights from this session. The questions are meant to help you reflect on truths related to each week's topic.

Day 1 – Philippians 1:11
The Fruit of Salvation
May you always be filled with the fruit of your salvation. (NLT)

Have you ever thought of joy as a natural result of salvation?

Day 2 – Matthew 6:20
More Than Stuff
Store your treasures in heaven, where moths and rust cannot destroy, and thieves do not break in and steal. (NLT)

Many people define happiness by their possessions, which can be broken or lost. Are there other reasons that make it futile to base our happiness (or joy) on stuff?

Day 3 – Proverbs 27:20
Never Satisfied
Just as Death and Destruction are never satisfied, so human desire is never satisfied. (NLT)

How does joy satisfy our needs in a way that happiness does not?

Day 4 – Luke 15:28-29
Circumstantial Happiness
The older brother was angry and wouldn't go in. His father came out and begged him, but he replied, 'All these years I've slaved for you and never once refused to do a single thing you told me to. And in all that time you never gave me even one young goat for a feast with my friends. (NLT)

The older brother's happiness was dependent upon circumstances – when those changed, he lost his happiness. How do your circumstances affect you?

Day 5 – Habakkuk 3:18
Rooted in the Truth
I will be joyful in the God of my salvation! (NLT)

Why do you think that joy must be rooted in the truth about who God is?

memory VERSE

Always be full of joy in the Lord. I say it again – rejoice!
Philippians 4:4 [NLT]

SESSION 2:
THE DNA OF RELATIONSHIPS

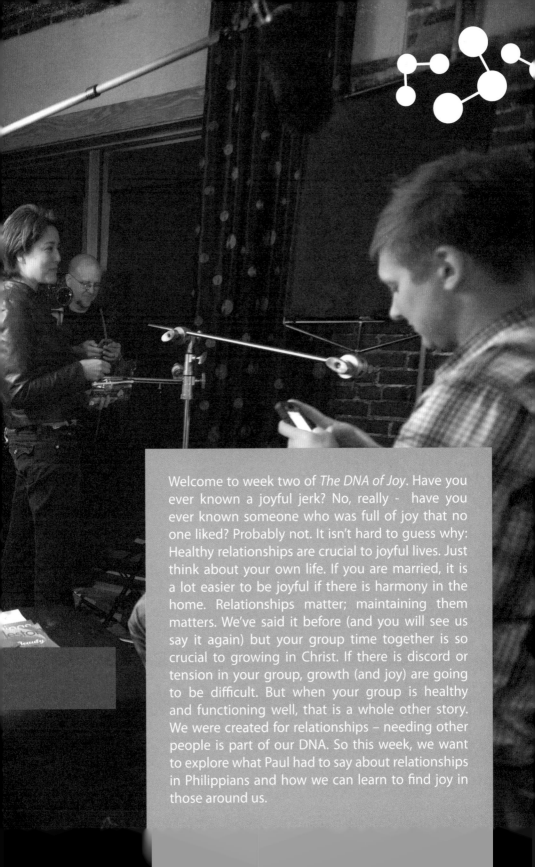

Welcome to week two of *The DNA of Joy*. Have you ever known a joyful jerk? No, really - have you ever known someone who was full of joy that no one liked? Probably not. It isn't hard to guess why: Healthy relationships are crucial to joyful lives. Just think about your own life. If you are married, it is a lot easier to be joyful if there is harmony in the home. Relationships matter; maintaining them matters. We've said it before (and you will see us say it again) but your group time together is so crucial to growing in Christ. If there is discord or tension in your group, growth (and joy) are going to be difficult. But when your group is healthy and functioning well, that is a whole other story. We were created for relationships – needing other people is part of our DNA. So this week, we want to explore what Paul had to say about relationships in Philippians and how we can learn to find joy in those around us.

small TALK

During each session, we will begin with a question or brief activity designed to "put us on the same page" for the session. If someone new has joined your group this week, please take a few minutes to introduce yourselves.

1 To see how well you know each other, try to guess the favorite movie (or maybe just genre) of someone else in your group.

2 For those who might be willing to share, what lasting idea from Session 1 has been on your mind this past week that you would be willing to mention to the rest of the group?

TEACHING

Throughout the sessions in *The DNA of Joy* we're hearing some teaching from Greg Surratt and learning what it means to find joy in everyday life. Learning about God in a group setting is one of the best ways to grow spiritually. It is especially relevant this week, as we look at the importance of relationships in our everyday lives. So let's move to the teaching portion of this section and learn about the DNA of Relationships:

PLAY DVD SESSION 2

Use the space to the right for notes, questions, or comments you want to bring up in the discussion later.

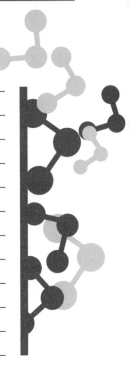

_____
_____
_____
_____
_____
_____
_____
_____
_____
_____
_____
_____
_____
_____
_____
_____
_____
_____
_____
_____
_____
_____
_____
_____
_____
_____
_____
_____
_____
_____
_____

REFLECT

In the questions that follow, you will review and expand on the teaching you just experienced.

1 Pastor Greg said that it is crucial to get the DNA of relationships right if we want to live joyful lives. Why do you think this is the case? Why are relationships so central to experiencing joy?

2 Paul had a terrible first experience at Philippi, but he chose to remember the people there with gratitude. Are there people or experiences in your past that are still robbing you of your joy? What would it take for you to begin practicing gratitude in those situations, to choose to have joy in the midst of pain?

3 Greg told a story about a relationship that went from bad to good because of prayer. Even though it was a difficult relationship, Greg began to pray for her and thank God for her. Over time, the relationship transformed. Have you ever experienced something similar? What could prayer do for the tough relationships in your life?

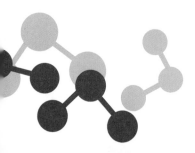

4 When we pray for other people, we might hope that God will change them. What happens instead is God changes us; he changes our hearts. What can we learn from that truth about living with and loving difficult people?

5 Read Philippians 1:6 aloud: "And I am sure that God, who began a good work in you will continue his work until it is finally finished on that day when Christ Jesus comes back again." What keeps us from being patient with other people? What would it take for us to be more patient, to trust in God to develop them in his time?

RESPOND

Now it's time to make some personal applications to all we've been thinking about in the last few minutes.

1 Greg talked about practicing gratitude, even during hard times. Do you practice gratitude? What is keeping you from being more grateful?

2 What difficult people in your life do you need to start praying for? Will you commit to begin praying for those people regularly? How might that change your relationships?

3 Hopefully your group is getting along well and growing together – maybe none of the "difficult" people in your life are in your group (as Greg said in the teaching, don't point!). Prayer doesn't make bad relationships good; it can also make good relationships great. Let's close in prayer, taking turns praying specifically for others in the group and beyond.

Close the session in prayer. Encourage each other to pray audibly for others in the group.

going DEEPER

You can explore the following Bible passages behind the teaching for this session as a group (if there is time) or on your own between sessions.

Read 1 Samuel 18:1-5 and 19:1-7. These verses tell some of the extraordinary story of the friendship between David (who would eventually be king of Israel) and Jonathan, son of Saul (the current king of Israel). Read the passages and consider the questions below.

1 What stands out to you about David and Jonathan's friendship?

2 Jonathan knew that David had been anointed Israel's future king by Samuel. That meant that David would be king after Saul, even though Jonathan was Saul's son. Jonathan could have been jealous, angry, or spiteful. Instead, we read that he loved David "as his own soul." How was he able to do this? Would you have been able to do the same, had you been in Jonathan's position?

3 What friendships have shaped your life? Reflect on how they influenced you and why they were so powerful.

daily REFLECTIONS

These are daily reviews of the key Bible verses and related others that will help you think about and apply the insights from this session. The questions are meant to help you reflect on truths related to each week's topic.

Day 1 – Genesis 2:18
Made for Relationship
Then the LORD God said, "It is not good for the man to be alone. I will make a helper who is just right for him." (NLT)

From the very beginning, we were designed by God for relationship. How can you see that design in yourself?

Day 2 – Ecclesiastes 4:12
Bonds of Friendship
A person standing alone can be attacked and defeated, but two can stand back-to-back and conquer. Three are even better, for a triple-braided cord is not easily broken. (NLT)

We are stronger when we are in relationship with others. How do the relationships in your life give you strength?

Day 3 – Matthew 5:44
Praying for Enemies
But I tell you, love your enemies and pray for those who persecute you. (NIV)

Are you praying for the difficult people in your life? How can you pray for them today?

Day 4 – Proverbs 27:6
Honest Friends
Wounds from a sincere friend are better than many kisses from an enemy. (NLT)

If given the choice, most of us would prefer an honest friend to a friend that would tell us what we want to hear. Why do you think that is?

Day 5 – 1 John 4:21
Loving God, Loving Others
And he has given us this command: Those who love God must also love their Christian brothers and sisters. (NLT)

We are told several times in the Bible that loving God means loving other people. Why does practicing the one naturally lead to the other?

memory VERSE

I thank my God every time I remember you. In all my prayers for all of you, I always pray with joy.
Philippians 1:3-4 [NIV]

SESSION 3:
THE DNA OF A GREAT BAD DAY

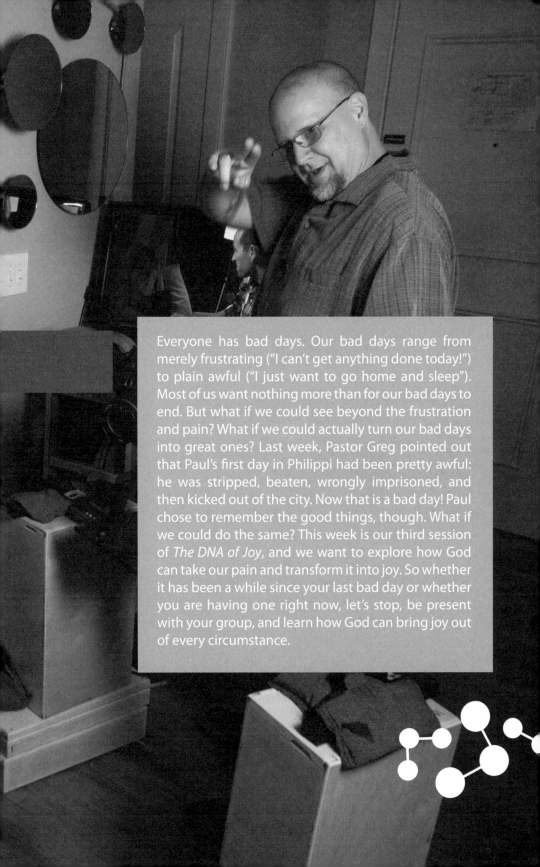

Everyone has bad days. Our bad days range from merely frustrating ("I can't get anything done today!") to plain awful ("I just want to go home and sleep"). Most of us want nothing more than for our bad days to end. But what if we could see beyond the frustration and pain? What if we could actually turn our bad days into great ones? Last week, Pastor Greg pointed out that Paul's first day in Philippi had been pretty awful: he was stripped, beaten, wrongly imprisoned, and then kicked out of the city. Now that is a bad day! Paul chose to remember the good things, though. What if we could do the same? This week is our third session of *The DNA of Joy*, and we want to explore how God can take our pain and transform it into joy. So whether it has been a while since your last bad day or whether you are having one right now, let's stop, be present with your group, and learn how God can bring joy out of every circumstance.

small TALK

During each session, we begin with a question or brief activity designed to "put us on the same page" for the session.

1 Today we will be talking about how to turn a bad day into a great one. We've all had some truly awful days in our lives. What was your worst bad day that you can look back on and laugh?

2 For those who might be joining us for the first time this session, who would like to describe one significant discovery you've made in the first two sessions that is already making a difference in your life?

TEACHING

Throughout the sessions in *The DNA of Joy* we're hearing some teaching from Greg Surratt and learning what it means to find joy in everyday life. Most of us just want our bad days to end. But we believe that God wants to transform our troubles into joy. That might seem farfetched to some of you, and that's ok! Just consider the possibility that a God who can do more than we could ask or imagine can also take our pain and turn it into joy. With that in mind, let's begin Greg's teaching for this session:

PLAY DVD SESSION 3

Use the space to the right for notes, questions, or comments you want to bring up in the discussion later.

REFLECT

1 During our bad days, we need to have a bigger perspective. In Philippians 1:12, Paul wrote that "everything that has happened to me has helped to spread the Good News." Paul was able to see the big picture even during hard times. What keeps us from doing that? Why is it so hard to maintain perspective during our bad days?

2 Greg talked about how photography taught him about focus. Once we have perspective, we need to remember what to focus on. Seeing the big picture is only helpful if you know what parts of the picture to look at. What happens in your life when you lose focus?

3 Paul was ready to go to heaven. In Philippians 1:21, Paul says that for him, dying and going to heaven would be even better than living. But in the next verse he says something very important. He says that as long as he is alive, he is going to be fruitful and have a purpose. What happens when we live our lives without purpose?

4 Greg gave us three things that should be a part of our mission in life: to worship God with our lives and bring glory to him; to encourage other believers; to share the Good News with those who haven't heard. Those are all things that we must grow into. If you were to describe your life right now, how would you fill in the blank: "For me to live is _____"?

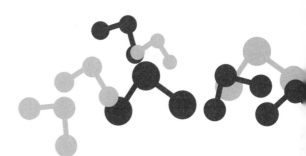

RESPOND

Now it's time to make some personal applications to all we've been thinking about in the last few minutes.

1 Consider for a moment: How do you typically deal with a bad day? Perhaps you could make a list of things you do. Which of these behaviors are helpful? Which are harmful?

2 Think back to those bad days. How could you have turned it around with perspective, focus, and mission? How can you prepare for your next bad day?

3 How can each of you be intentional about encouraging the people in your life when they are having a bad day?

4 Go around your group – is anyone anticipating having a bad day this week? If so, how can your group support them?

Close the session in prayer. Encourage each other to pray audibly for others in the group.

going DEEPER

You can explore the following Bible passages behind the teaching for this session as a group (if there is time) or on your own between sessions.

Read Psalm 30. Many of the Psalms are joyful; others are sad, or angry. In Psalm 30, David gives thanks to God for bringing him up out of a bad day. He acknowledges that hard times come but he points out that God has always turned those times into joy.

1 In verse 2, David says that he cried out to God for help. When you are in trouble or having a bad day, is your natural response to go to God for help? If so, what have you learned as a result? If not, what is your natural response and why do you think that is?

2 Some people see relying on God as a crutch; a last resort for people who aren't strong enough to deal with difficult times. But David says that his reliance on God has made him "as secure as a mountain." Why do you think some people are reluctant to trust in God?

3 Have you ever experienced God turning your "mourning into joyful dancing?"

daily REFLECTIONS

These are daily reviews of the key Bible verses and related others that will help you think about and apply the insights from this session. The questions are meant to help you reflect on truths related to each week's topic.

Day 1 – 2 Corinthians 4:8
Standing Strong
We are pressed on every side by troubles, but we are not crushed. We are perplexed, but not driven to despair. (NLT)

When we experience a bad day, where do we get our strength? Do we try to endure it on our own, or do we rely on God to sustain us?

Day 2 – 1 Peter 5:7
God Cares
Give all your worries and cares to God, for he cares about you. (NLT)

God is sensitive to our troubles – when we have a bad day, he wants us to come to him. Do you see God as a sympathetic father during those times?

Day 3 – Matthew 6:34
Keep Your Focus
"So don't worry about tomorrow, for tomorrow will bring its own worries. Today's trouble is enough for today." (NIV)

When we are worried or having a bad day, it can be easy to lose our focus. Why do you think Jesus's encouragement to not worry about tomorrow is so important?

Day 4 – 2 Corinthians 12:9
Powerful Weaknesses
"My grace is all you need. My power works best in weakness." (NLT)

Paul wanted God to take some of his trouble away – the verse above was God's response. What is God trying to teach you in the midst of your pain?

Day 5 – James 1:2
Bad Day, Great Opportunity
Dear brothers and sisters, when troubles come your way, consider it an opportunity for great joy. (NLT)

What might happen if you started viewing your bad days as opportunities for your greatest joy?

memory VERSE

… I rejoice. And I will continue to rejoice.
Philippians 1:18 [NLT]

SESSION 4:
THE DNA OF PERSEVERANCE

By this point we should be settling into a level of comfort with the group, continuing to welcome any newcomers. Your group has reached the halfway point of this study – congratulations! It is fitting, because in Session 4 we will be taking a look at the DNA of perseverance. This session is about keeping our joy no matter what.

The Bible has a lot to say about perseverance, as you'll see in the content for this session. Perseverance is about more than just keeping our head down and enduring, or just waiting until things get better. We persevere because we have a God who stands with us, who is beside us in every circumstance. That is why perseverance isn't mere endurance; it is a victorious confidence, a certainty that with God's help, we will prevail. Now that is a reason to be joyful!

small TALK

During each session, we begin with a question or brief activity designed to "put us on the same page" for the session.

1 This session is about keeping our joy, no matter what. Does anyone in your group have a story about finding joy in unexpected places or circumstances?

2 If someone has an insight that they gained from last week that has been on their minds, ask if they would like to share with the group.

TEACHING

Throughout the sessions in The DNA of Joy we're hearing some teaching from Greg Surratt and learning what it means to find joy in everyday life. Today, we want to talk about how we can keep our joy no matter what. Let's begin our teaching from Greg for this session and see what God wants to say to each one of us:

PLAY DVD SESSION 4

Use the space to the right for notes, questions, or comments you want to bring up in the discussion later.

REFLECT

In the questions that follow, you will review and expand on the teaching you just experienced.

1 Pastor Greg points out that losing things can steal our joy. Why is that? What is an example from your own life of something you lost that robbed you of your joy?

2 It is vital to remember that God is always good. In our hardest times, that is a truth that we can cling to. When we remember that God is good, we can deal with our doubts and remember who we know God to be. Do you have a hard time remembering that God is good? What is your default setting?

3 Greg talks about legalism and why it is dangerous. Why do you think it can be so easy for people to drift into legalism? Why is legalism attractive?

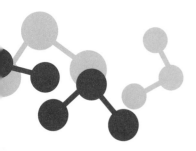

4 Knowing Jesus changes everything. It's the only thing that truly matters in the end. It is the only thing that can help us keep our joy. Paul says that compared to knowing Christ, everything else is garbage. What has knowing Jesus meant in your life?

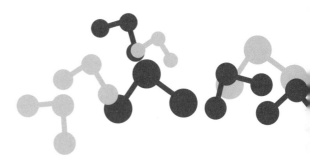

RESPOND

Now it's time to make some personal applications to all we've been thinking about in the last few minutes.

1 Do you believe that God is good all the time? It can be hard to remember that, especially during troubling times. What can you do to make sure that in all situations you are reminded of that simple truth?

2 What has been stealing your joy lately? What steps can you take to change that?

3 If knowing Jesus changes everything, shouldn't it continually change us? In other words, knowing Jesus means constantly changing, constantly becoming more like him. Discuss how your group can keep each other accountable this week with this simple question: How is knowing Jesus changing you today?your life when they are having a bad day?

4 Check in with your spiritual partner(s), or with another partner if yours is absent. Share something God taught you during your time in His Word this week, or read a brief section from your journal. Be sure to write down your partner's progress on page 82.

Close the session in prayer. Encourage each other to pray audibly for others in the group.

going DEEPER

You can explore the following Bible passages behind the teaching for this session as a group (if there is time) or on your own between sessions.

Read Psalm 4. This Psalm of David calls upon God to hear his prayer. He wants to know that God is listening, that God knows what is happening. David knows that God is good and he wants God to know that he trusts him. Read this Psalm and spend some time reflecting on it before moving on to the questions below.

1 What is David's response to the people who want to harm him and harm his reputation?

2 David knows that anger robs us of joy – he writes that we should wait a day and think about things before acting. What happens to our anger when we make ourselves wait to act?

3 Others point to their own work as the source of their happiness – David relies on God alone for joy. Do you ever find yourself relying on your own strength and abilities for your joy?

4 What stands out most to you in this passage?

daily REFLECTIONS

These are daily reviews of the key Bible verses and related others that will help you think about and apply the insights from this session. The questions are meant to help you reflect on truths related to each week's topic.

Day 1 – Job 19:25
God Prevails
But as for me, I know that my Redeemer lives, and he will stand upon the earth at last. (NLT)

Job knew that no matter the circumstances, God is good, all the time. Do you believe that?

Day 2 – Romans 8:23
Someday…
And we believers also groan, even though we have the Holy Spirit within us as a foretaste of future glory, for we long for our bodies to be released from sin and suffering. (NLT)

Our perseverance is based on the good promises of God. Which of God's promises are most encouraging to you?

Day 3 – Habakkuk 2:4
A New Way to Live
But the righteous will live by their faithfulness to God. (NIV)

If knowing Jesus changes everything, how can you better reflect this truth today?

Day 4 – 1 Corinthians 9:24

Run!

Don't you realize that in a race everyone runs, but only one person gets the prize? So run to win! (NLT)

Sometimes perseverance, keeping our joy, means aggressively pursuing God. How can you pursue God today?

Day 5 – James 1:3-4

Needing Nothing

For you know that when your faith is tested, your endurance has a chance to grow. So let it grow, for when your endurance is fully developed, you will be perfect and complete, needing nothing. (NLT)

When we are tested, when we are about to lose our joy, relying on God builds our endurance. Reflect on this passage and be encouraged knowing this truth: God uses hard times to make you stronger.

memory VERSE

Whatever happens, dear brothers and sisters, may the Lord give you joy.

Philippians 3:1 [NLT]

SESSION 5:
THE DNA OF CONTENTMENT

Contentment – doesn't that sound nice? We talked about happiness in the first session and about how elusive and fleeting it is. Contentment is different; we all want to be content. The problem is that no one seems to know what it means. What does being content look like? As soon as we think we know, we aren't content anymore! The apostle Paul told the Philippians that he had found the secret of contentment and that is what we want to explore in this fifth session of *The DNA of Joy*.

small TALK

During each session, we begin with a question or brief activity designed to "put us on the same page" for the session.

1 Go around the group and have each person describe what a perfect day would look like for them.

2 What does contentment mean to you? What would a content life look like? Why is defining contentment so hard?

TEACHING

Throughout the sessions in The DNA of Joy we're hearing some teaching from Greg Surratt and learning what it means to find joy in everyday life. We've reached Session 5 – we're in the home stretch. Hopefully this study has been a time of great fellowship and growth within your group. But (this session's topic aside!) we don't want you to be content with your progress just yet! Let's begin the teaching now and listen with open hearts:

PLAY DVD SESSION 5

Use the space to the right for notes, questions, or comments you want to bring up in the discussion later.

REFLECT

In the questions that follow, you will review and expand on the teaching you just experienced.

1 Take a moment and read Philippians 4:10-13. Paul says that he has found the secret of contentment. Does his explanation seem simplistic to you?

2 What about Pastor Greg's statement that "contentment is found in wanting what you already have, not in pursuing what you want." Have you experienced that in your own life?

3 Stewardship is about remembering that everything belongs to God. Why is that so hard? How can we find a balance between being good stewards and enjoying what God has given to us?

4 Greg told the story of Marcinius, the monk, who lived in the desert to get away from the distractions of the world. When he came back to civilization, he said "My heart leapt with joy within me, with all of the things that I saw but did not need." Reflect on that statement for a moment with your group. How does that view compare to our culture? Are we trained to practice gratitude, or want more stuff?

5 The last word is surrender. Where are you discontent? What would surrender look like in that area of your life?

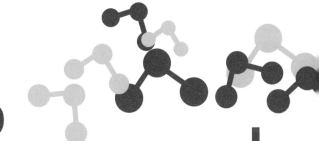

RESPOND

Now it's time to make some personal applications to all we've been thinking about in the last few minutes.

1 What is the biggest obstacle between you and contentment? How can you overcome that obstacle? What do you need to surrender to God this week?

2 Since this is our next-to-last session in this series, what have we decided about next steps? What are some topics or questions that you would like to explore in the future with this or another small group?

3 Take a few minutes to discuss the future of your group. How many of you are willing to stay together as a group and work through another study together? If you have time, turn to the Small Group Agreement on page 77 and talk about any changes you would like to make as you move forward as a group.

Close the session in prayer. Encourage each other to pray audibly for others in the group.

going DEEPER

You can explore the following Bible passages behind the teaching for this session as a group (if there is time) or on your own between sessions.

Read Mark 10:17-27. This passage tells the story of a man who had a conversation with Jesus. In fact, at the end of their talk, Jesus extended a personal invitation to the man to come and follow him. The man went away disappointed.

1 Mark tells us that the man "went away sad, for he had many possessions." Do you think you would have made a different decision if you were in that man's place?

2 Jesus told the man to give away everything he had – but he couldn't. Paul said that he had learned the secret of living with much and with little. This man had only learned how to live with much. Contentment is not just having what we want; it is also about being joyful when we have none of what we want. Why is it so hard to be joyful when we don't have things we want?

3 Who do you think struggles more with contentment: the rich or the poor? Why?

daily REFLECTIONS

These are daily reviews of the key Bible verses and related others that will help you think about and apply the insights from this session. The questions are meant to help you reflect on truths related to each week's topic.

Day 1 – Psalm 23:1
Contentment
The Lord is my shepherd; I have all that I need. (NLT)

Do you see God as the supplier of all your needs?

Day 2 – Matthew 6:31-32
Do Not Worry
"So don't worry about these things, saying, 'What will we eat? What will we drink? What will we wear?' These things dominate the thoughts of unbelievers, but your heavenly Father already knows all your needs." (NLT)

Do you trust God to provide for you?

Day 3 – Ecclesiastes 1:8
The Opposite of Content
No matter how much we see, we are never satisfied. No matter how much we hear, we are not content. (NIV)

Why can the things of this world never make us content? Why are we never satisfied apart from God?

Day 4 – Philippians 4:6
Talk to God
Don't worry about anything; instead, pray about everything. Tell God what you need, and thank him for all he has done. (NLT)

When you think of what God has already done for you, does it give you confidence in the future?

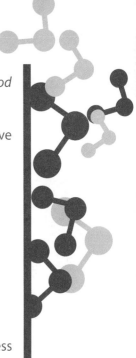

Day 5 – 1 Timothy 6:6
True Wealth
Yet true godliness with contentment is itself great wealth. NLT)

Why do you think so few people see value (wealth) in godliness and in being content with God?

memory VERSE

I have learned the secret of living in every situation, whether it is with a full stomach or empty, with plenty or little. For I can do everything through Christ, who gives me strength.
Philippians 4:12-13 [NLT]

SESSION 6:
THE DNA OF GIVING

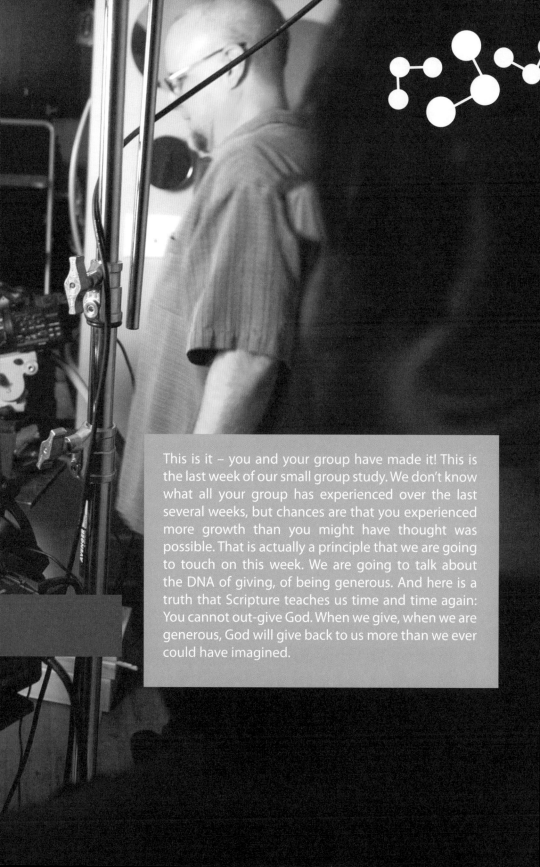

This is it – you and your group have made it! This is the last week of our small group study. We don't know what all your group has experienced over the last several weeks, but chances are that you experienced more growth than you might have thought was possible. That is actually a principle that we are going to touch on this week. We are going to talk about the DNA of giving, of being generous. And here is a truth that Scripture teaches us time and time again: You cannot out-give God. When we give, when we are generous, God will give back to us more than we ever could have imagined.

small TALK

In this final session of the series we are coming face to face with the choice we have been considering: What kind of life will we live. A life that finds joy in the everyday small things is a joy that sees God everywhere.

1 What would you say is one unforgettable idea that you are taking away from the last five sessions of The DNA of Joy?

2 Why do you think giving matters? Why do we encourage people to be generous?

TEACHING

Throughout the sessions in The DNA of Joy we're hearing some teaching from Greg Surratt and learning what it means to find joy in everyday life. In this final week of the series, we should see some of the long term implications of applying the DNA of joy in our own lives. And we should be able to see some results of earlier lessons. With that possibility in mind, let's begin our teaching for this session with Pastor Greg Surratt:

PLAY DVD SESSION 6

Use the space to the right for notes, questions, or comments you want to bring up in the discussion later.

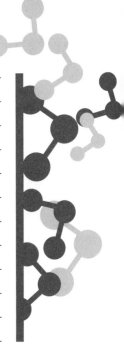

REFLECT

1 Read Luke 6:38. God promises that he will supply all of our needs, but he wants us to give and be generous. He says that he will reward our generosity. Why do you think our giving matters so much to God? The verse tells us that however we give to others, that is how God will give to us. Does that truth make you stop and reconsider your generosity towards those around you?

2 Do you tend to ask "how much should I give" or "how much should I keep"?

3 Paul talked about generosity as being a "sweet-smelling sacrifice" that God is pleased with. Have you ever thought about whether your giving smelled good? Have some fun in your group – rate the smell of your giving lately.

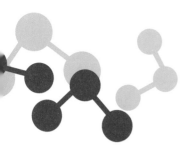

4 Reflect on the last six weeks. Have you seen your life impacted by these sessions? How has this study transformed your understanding of joy?

RESPOND

At this point we move in our discussion from talking about implications of the teaching to application of the teaching. If we grasp what the idea means we can talk about what it means in our lives.

1 What can you do to be generous this week? It doesn't have to involve money – it can involve your time or your talents. Brainstorm in your group some ways that each of you can be generous to those around you over the next several days.

2 Describe to the rest of the group one specific step you are taking to make the DNA of joy present in your everyday life.

3 Before you talk about them, take a few minutes to jot down three specific action steps related to this entire series that would move you further on the journey toward being joyful every day. These should be matters others in the group can pray about for you.

a _____

b _____

c _____

4 Now share at least one of these, if not all three, with the rest of the group to create a point of accountability, and give the group permission to ask you about your progress in this or these steps.

Close the session in prayer. Encourage each other to pray audibly for others in the group.

going DEEPER

You can explore the following Bible passages behind the teaching for this session as a group (if there is time) or on your own between sessions.

Read Mark 12:41-44. This is a very well-known story. Jesus and his disciples were sitting in a synagogue one day. They were watching people and they saw a lot of the rich people put in large amounts of money. Probably, those people were making sure that everyone nearby saw exactly how much money they gave. Then a little old woman came and put a few pennies in the box.

1 What does this passage teach about giving?

2 Can a person give a lot and still be stingy? Why isn't giving a lot of money the same thing as being generous?

3 The widow's generosity was inconvenient – Jesus said that she gave everything she had. Did she demonstrate a radical trust in God, or an irresponsibility with her finances?

4 What would inconvenient generosity look like in your life?

daily REFLECTIONS

These are daily reviews of the key Bible verses and related others that will help you think about and apply the insights from this session. The questions are meant to help you reflect on truths related to each week's topic.

Day 1 – Isaiah 32:8
Generous People
But generous people plan to do what is generous, and they stand firm in their generosity. (NLT)

What does your giving say about the kind of person you are?

Day 2 – Deuteronomy 15:8
Loving the Poor
But if there are any poor Israelites in your towns when you arrive in the land the LORD your God is giving you, do not be hard-hearted or tightfisted toward them. Instead, be generous and lend them whatever they need. (NLT)

Does our culture tend to treat the poor with understanding and generosity? Why or why not?

Day 3 – Psalm 37:21
The Godly
The wicked borrow and never repay, but the godly are generous givers. (NIV)

Do you see generous giving as a hallmark of knowing God?

Day 4 – Ephesians 4:28
From Thief to Giver
If you are a thief, quit stealing. Instead, use your hands for good hard work, and then give generously to others in need. (NLT)

Does your giving flow directly out of your work?

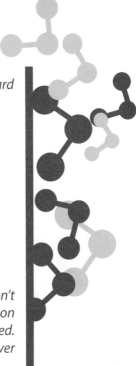

Day 5 – 2 Corinthians 9:7-8
Cheerful Givers
You must each decide in your heart how much to give. And don't give reluctantly or in response to pressure. "For God loves a person who gives cheerfully." And God will generously provide all you need. Then you will always have everything you need and plenty left over to share with others. (NLT)

Is your giving cheerful? Do you really believe that if you give generously, you will have plenty left over?

memory VERSE

And my God will meet all your needs according to the riches of his glory in Christ Jesus.
Philippians 4:19 [NLT]

APPENDIX

GREAT RESOURCES TO MAKE YOUR SMALL GROUP EVEN BETTER!

frequently
ASKED QUESTIONS

What do we do on the first night of our group?

Like all fun things in life–have a party! A "get to know you" coffee, dinner, or dessert is a great way to launch a new study. You may want to review the Group Agreement (page 77) and share the names of a few friends you can invite to join you. But most importantly, have fun before your study time begins.

Where do we find new members for our group?

This can be troubling, especially for new groups that have only a few people or for existing groups that lose a few people along the way. We encourage you to pray with your group and then brainstorm a list of people from work, church, your neighborhood, your children's school, family, the gym, etc.. Then have each group member invite some of the people on his or her list.

No matter how you find members, try to stay on the lookout for new people to join your group. All groups tend to go through healthy attrition– the result of moves, releasing new leaders, ministry opportunities, and so forth–and if the group gets too small, it could be at risk of shutting down. If you and your group stay open, you'll be amazed at the people God sends your way. The next person just might become a friend for life. You never know!

How long will this group meet?

It's totally up to the group. Most groups meet weekly for at least their first 6 weeks, but every other week can work as well. We strongly recommend that the group meet for the first six months on a weekly basis if possible. This allows for continuity, and if people miss a meeting they aren't gone for a whole month.

At the end of this study, each group member will decide if he or she wants to continue on for another 6-week study. Some groups launch relationships for years to come, and others are stepping-stones into another group experience. Either way, enjoy the journey.

Can we do this study on our own?

Absolutely! This may sound crazy but one of the best ways to do this study is not with a full house but with a few friends. You may choose to gather with one other couple who would enjoy going to the movies or having a quiet dinner and then walking through this study. Jesus will be with you even if there are only two of you (Matthew 18:20).

What if this group is not working for us?

You're not alone! This could be the result of a personality conflict, life stage difference, geographical distance, level of spiritual maturity, or any number of things. Relax. Pray for God's direction, and at the end of this 6-week study, decide whether to continue with this group or find another. You don't buy the first car you test drive or marry the first person you date, and the same goes with a group. Don't bail out before the 6 weeks are up–God might have something to teach you. Also, don't run from conflict or prejudge people before you have given them a chance. God is still working in you too!

Who is the leader?

Most groups have an official leader. But ideally, the group will mature and members will rotate the leadership of meetings. We have discovered that healthy groups rotate hosts/leaders and homes on a regular basis. This model ensures that all members grow, give their unique contribution, and develop their gifts. This study guide and the Holy Spirit can keep things on track even when you rotate leaders. Christ has promised to be in your midst as you gather. Ultimately, God is your leader each step of the way.

How do we handle the child care needs in our group?

Very carefully. Seriously, this can be a sensitive issue. We suggest that you empower the group to openly brainstorm solutions. You may try one option that works for a while and then adjust over time. Our favorite approach is for adults to meet in the living room or dining room, and to share the cost of a babysitter (or two) who can be with the kids in a different part of the house. In this way, parents don't have to be away from their children all evening when their children are too young to be left at home. A second option is to use one home for the kids and a second home (close by or a phone call away) for the adults. A third idea is to rotate the responsibility of providing a lesson or care for the children either in the same home or in another home nearby. This can be an incredible blessing for kids. Finally, the most common idea is to decide that you need to have a night to invest in your spiritual lives individually or as a couple, and to make your own arrangements for child care. No matter what decision the group makes, the best approach is to dialogue openly about both the problem and the solution.

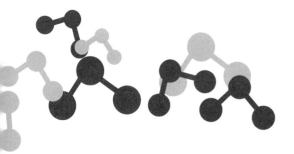

small group
AGREEMENT

Our Purpose

To provide a safe environment where participants experience authentic community and spiritual growth.

Our Values

Group Attendance	To give priority to the group meeting. We will call or email if we will be late or absent. (Completing the Group Calendar on page 79 will minimize this issue.)
Safe Environment	To help create a safe place where people can be heard and feel loved. (Please, no quick answers, snap judgments, or simple fixes.)
Respect Differences	To be gentle and gracious toward people with different spiritual maturity, personal opinions, temperaments, or "imperfections" in fellow group members. We are all works in progress.
Confidentiality	To keep anything that is shared strictly confidential and within the group, and to avoid sharing improper information about those outside the group.
Encouragement for Growth	To be not just takers but givers of life. We want to spiritually multiply our life by serving others with our God-given gifts.
Shared Ownership	To remember that every member is a minister and to ensure that each attender will share a small team role or responsibility over time. (See the Team Roles on page 80.)
Rotating Hosts/ Leaders and Homes	To encourage different people to host the group in their homes, and to rotate the responsibility of facilitating each meeting. (See the Group Calendar on page 79.)

Our Times Together

Refreshments/mealtimes

Childcare

When we will meet (day of week)

Where we will meet (place)

We will begin at (time)   and end at

We will do our best to have some or all of us attend a worship service together. Our primary worship service time will be

Date of this agreement

Date we will review this agreement again

Who (other than the leader) will review this agreement at the end of this study

group
CALENDAR

Planning and calendaring can help ensure the greatest participation at every meeting. At the end of each meeting, review this calendar. Be sure to include a regular rotation of host homes and leaders, and don't forget birthdays, socials, church events, holidays, and mission/ministry projects.

Date	Lesson	Host Home	Dessert/ Meal	Leader
4/7	1	Steve and Laura's	Joe	Bill

team
ROLES

The Bible makes clear that every member, not just the small group leader, is a minister in the body of Christ. In a healthy small group, every member takes on some small role or responsibility. It's more fun and effective if you team up on these roles.

Review the team roles and responsibilities below, and have each member volunteer for a role or participate on a team. If someone doesn't know where to serve or is holding back, have the group suggest a team or role. It's best to have one or two people on each team so you have each of the five purposes covered. Serving in even a small capacity will not only help your leader but also will make the group more fun for everyone. Don't hold back. Join a team!

The opportunities below are broken down by the five purposes and then by a crawl (beginning step), walk (intermediate step), or run (advanced step). Try to cover at least the crawl and walk roles, and select a role that matches your group, your gifts, and your maturity.

CONNECTING TEAM
fellowship & community building

Crawl:
Host a social event or group activity in the first week or two.

_____
_____
_____

Walk:
Create a list of friends and invite them to an open house or group social.

_____
_____
_____

Run:
Plan a twenty-four-hour retreat or weekend getaway for the group. Lead the connecting time each week for the group.

_____
_____
_____

GROWING TEAM
discipleship & spiritual growth

Crawl:
Coordinate the spiritual partners for the group. Facilitate a three- or four-person discussion circle during the Bible study portion of your meeting. Coordinate the discussion circles.

Walk:
Tabulate the Personal Health Assessments (spiritualhealth.seacoast.org) in a summary to let people know how you're doing as a group. Encourage personal devotions through group discussions and pairing up with spiritual (accountability) partners.

Run:
Take the group on a prayer walk, or plan a day of solitude, fasting, or personal retreat.

_____
_____
_____

SERVING TEAM
discovering your God-given design for ministry

Crawl:
Ensure that every member finds a group role or team that he or she enjoys.

Walk:
Have each member take a gift test (5fold.seacoast.org) and determine your group's gifts. Plan a ministry project together.

Run:
Help each member decide on a way to use his or her unique gifts somewhere in the church.

_____
_____
_____

SHARING TEAM
sharing & evangelism

Crawl:
Coordinate the group's Prayer and Praise Report of friends and family who don't know Christ.

Walk:
Search for group mission opportunities and plan a cross-cultural group activity.

Run:
Take a small-group "vacation" to host a six-week group in your neighborhood or office. Then come back together with your current group.

_____
_____
_____

WORSHIP TEAM
surrendering your heart to worship

Crawl:
Maintain the group's Prayer and Praise Report or journal.

Walk:
Lead a brief time of worship each week (at the beginning or end of your meeting), either a cappella or using a song from a worship CD.

Run:
Plan a unique time of worship through Communion, night of prayer, or nature walking.

_____
_____
_____

spiritual partners'
CHECK-IN PAGE

Briefly check in each week and write down your personal plans and progress targets for the next week (or even for the next few weeks). This could be done (before or after the meeting) on the phone, through an e-mail message or even in person from time to time.

My Name:

- -

Spiritual Partner's Name:

	Our Plan	Our Progress
Week 1		
Week 2		
Week 3		
Week 4		
Week 5		

small group
ROSTER

Name	Address	Phone	Email

memory
VERSES

Session 1

(Philippians 4:4 NLT)
Always be full of joy in the Lord. I say it again – rejoice!

Session 2

(Philippians 1:3-4 NIV)
I thank my God every time I remember you. In all my prayers for all of you, I always pray with joy.

Session 3

(Philippians 1:18 NLT)
… I rejoice. And I will continue to rejoice.

Session 4

(Philippians 3:1 NLT)
Whatever happens, dear brothers and sisters, may the Lord give you joy.

Session 5

(Philippians 4:12-13 NLT)
I have learned the secret of living in every situation, whether it is with a full stomach or empty, with plenty or little. For I can do everything through Christ, who gives me strength.

Session 6

(Philippians 4:19 NIV)
And my God will meet all your needs according to the riches of his glory in Christ Jesus.

prayer and
PRAISE REPORT

	Prayer Requests	Praise Reports
Week 1		
Week 2		
Week 3		
Week 4		
Week 5		
Week 6		

hosting an
OPEN HOUSE

If you're starting a new group, try planning an "open house" before your first formal group meeting. Even if you only have two to four core members, it's a great way to break the ice and to consider prayerfully who else might be open to join you over the next few weeks. You can also use this kick-off meeting to hand out study guides, spend some time getting to know each other, discuss each person's expectations for the group, and briefly pray for each other.

A simple meal or good desserts always make a kick-off meeting more fun. After people introduce themselves and share how they ended up being at the meeting, have everyone respond to a few icebreaker questions: "What is your favorite family vacation?" or "What is one thing you love about your church/our community?" or "What are three things about your life growing up that most people here don't know?" Next, ask everyone to tell what he or she hopes to get out of the study. You might want to review the Small Group Agreement and talk about each person's expectations and priorities.

You can skip this kick-off meeting if your time is limited, but you'll experience a huge benefit if you take the time to connect with each other in this way.

leading for the
FIRST TIME

1 Sweaty palms are a healthy sign. The Bible says God is gracious to the humble. Remember who is in control; the time to worry is when you're not worried. Those who are soft in heart (and sweaty palmed) are those whom God is sure to speak through.

2 Seek support. Ask your leader, co-leader, or close friend to pray for you and prepare with you before the session. Walking through the study will help you anticipate potentially difficult questions and discussion topics.

3 Bring your uniqueness to the study. Lean into who you are and how God wants you to uniquely lead the study.

4 Prepare. Prepare. Prepare. Go through the session several times. If you are using the DVD, listen to the teaching segment and Leadership Lifter. Consider writing in a journal or fasting for a day to prepare yourself for what God wants to do.

5 Don't wait until the last minute to get everything ready.

6 Ask for feedback so you can grow. Perhaps in an email or on cards handed out at the study, have everyone write down three things you did well and one thing you could improve on. Don't get defensive; instead, show an openness to learn and grow.

7 Prayerfully consider launching a new group. This doesn't need to happen overnight, but God's heart is for this to happen over time. Not all Christians are called to be leaders or teachers, but we are all called to be "shepherds" of a few someday.

8 Share with your group what God is doing in your heart. God is searching for those whose hearts are fully his. Share your trials and victories. We promise that people will relate.

9 Prayerfully consider whom you would like to pass the baton to next week. It's only fair. God is ready for the next member of your group to go on the faith journey you just traveled. Make it fun, and expect God to do the rest.

small group
LEADERSHIP 101

Congratulations! You have responded to the call to help shepherd Jesus' flock. There are a few other tasks in the family of God that are as challenging, rewarding, and humbling as this. As you prepare to lead, whether it is one session or the entire series, here are a few thoughts to keep in mind. We encourage you to read these and review them with each new discussion leader before he or she leads.

1. Remember that you are not alone.
God knows everything about you, and He knew that you would be asked to lead your group. Remember that it is common for all good leaders to feel that they are not ready to lead. Moses, Solomon, Jeremiah and Timothy - they all were reluctant to lead. God promises, "Never will I leave you; never will I forsake you" (Hebrews 13:5). Whether you are leading for one evening, for several weeks, or for a lifetime, you will be blessed as you serve.

2. Don't try to do it alone.
Pray right now for God to help you build a healthy leadership team. If you can enlist a co-leader to help you lead the group, you will find your experience to be much richer. This is your chance to involve as many people as you can in building a healthy group. All you have to do is call and ask people to help; you'll be surprised at the response.

3. Just be yourself.
Your group needs you to be you! God wants you to use your unique gifts and temperament. Don't try to do things exactly like another leader; do them in a way that fits you! Just admit it when you don't have an answer, and apologize when you make a mistake. Your group will love you for it, and you'll sleep better at night!

4. Prepare for your meeting ahead of time.

Review the session and the leader's notes, and write down your responses to each question. Pay special attention to exercises that ask group members to do something other than engage in discussion.

These exercises will help your group live what the Bible teaches, not just talk about it. Be sure you understand how an exercise works, and bring any necessary supplies (such as paper and pens) to your meeting. If the exercise employs one of the items in the appendix, be sure to look over that item so you'll know how it works. Finally, review "Outline for Each Session" so you'll remember the purpose of each section in the study.

5. Pray for your group members by name.

Before you begin your session, go around the room in your mind and pray for each member by name. You may want to review the prayer list at least once a week. Ask God to use your time together to touch the heart of every person uniquely. Expect God to lead you to whomever He wants you to encourage or challenge in a special way. If you listen, God will surely lead!

6. When you ask a question, be patient.

Someone will eventually respond. Sometimes people need a moment or two of silence to think about the question, and if silence doesn't bother you, it won't bother anyone else. After someone responds, affirm the response with a simple "thanks" or "I appreciate you sharing that." Then ask, "How about somebody else?" or "Would someone who hasn't shared like to add anything?" Be sensitive to new people or reluctant members who aren't ready to say, pray or do anything. If you give them a safe setting, they will open up over time.

7. Provide transitions between questions.

When guiding the discussion, always read aloud the transitional paragraphs and the questions. Ask the group if anyone would like to read the paragraph or Bible passage. Don't call on anyone, but ask for a volunteer, and then be patient until someone begins. Be sure to thank the person who reads aloud.

8. Break up into small groups each week, or they won't stay.

If your group has more than seven people, we strongly encourage you to gather in discussion circles of three or four people during the REFLECT or RESPOND sections of the study. With a greater opportunity to talk in a small circle, people will connect more with the study, apply more quickly what they're learning and ultimately get more out of it. A small circle also encourages a quiet person to participate and tends to minimize the effects of a more vocal or dominant member. It can also help people feel more loved in your group. When you gather again at the end of the section, you can have one person summarize the highlights from each circle. Small circles are also helpful during prayer time. People who are unaccustomed to praying aloud will feel more comfortable trying it with just two or three others. Also, prayer requests won't take as long, so circles will have more time to actually pray. When you gather back with the whole group, you can have one person from each circle briefly update everyone on the prayer requests. People are more willing to pray in small circles if they know that the whole group will hear all of the prayer requests.

9. Rotate facilitators weekly.

At the end of each meeting, ask the group who should lead the following week. Let the group help select your weekly facilitator. You may be perfectly capable of leading each time, but you will help others grow in their faith and gifts if you give them opportunities to lead. You can use the Small Group Calendar to fill in the names of all meeting leaders at once if you prefer.

10. One final challenge (for new or first time leaders):

Before your first opportunity to lead, look up each of the five passages listed below. Read each one as a devotional exercise to help equip yourself with a shepherd's heart. Trust us on this one. If you do this, you will be more than ready for your first meeting.

Matthew 9:36
1 Peter 5:2-4
Psalm 23
Ezekiel 34:11-16
1 Thessalonians 2:7-8, 11-12

GREG SURRATT

Greg is the founding pastor of Seacoast Church, one of the early adopters of the multisite model and author of *Ir-Rev-Rend*. Located in Mt. Pleasant, South Carolina, Seacoast has been recognized by various media as an innovative and influential thought leader in future strategies for church growth and development. Seacoast combines a unique approach to highly participatory worship with a heart for missional evangelism. Greg calls their weekends a "practical, spirit-filled, but non-spooky, yet kind of mystical worship experience, done in multiple locations, very inexpensively." Seacoast currently has 32 weekend worship experiences in 12 separate locations.

Greg is also a founding board member of the Association of Related Churches (ARC) arcchurches.com, a church planting network that has given birth to over 300 churches in the last 11 years. Greg is married to a very hip grandma, has 4 children, 10 grandchildren, and enjoys reading, photography, fishing, golfing, and rooting for lost causes… specifically the Cubs, Broncos, and Gamecocks.